EFFECTIVE COMMUNICATION

Communication Skills

Learn How To Be More Proficient and Effective In Your Communications With Friends, Family and Associates.

Chase Kaiser

Published by:

Dana Publishing
P.O. Box 1801
Mentor, OH 44060

<u>**Legal & Disclaimer**</u>

The information contained in this book and its contents is not designed to replace or take the place of any form of medical or professional advice; and is not meant to replace the need for independent medical, financial, legal or other professional advice or services, as may be required. The content and information in this book has been provided for educational and entertainment purposes only.

The content and information contained in this book has been compiled from sources deemed reliable, and it is accurate to the best of the Author's knowledge, information and belief. However, the Author cannot guarantee its accuracy and validity and cannot be held liable for any errors and/or omissions. Further, changes are periodically made to this book as and when needed. Where appropriate and/or necessary, you must consult a professional (including but not limited to your doctor, attorney, financial advisor or such other professional advisor) before using any of the suggested remedies, techniques, or information in this book.

Upon using the contents and information contained in this book, you agree to hold harmless the Author from and against any damages, costs, and expenses, including any legal fees potentially resulting from the application of any of the information provided by this book. This disclaimer applies to any loss, damages or injury caused by the use and application, whether directly or indirectly, of any advice or information presented, whether for breach of contract, tort, negligence, personal injury, criminal intent, or under any other cause of action.

You agree to accept all risks of using the information presented inside this book.You agree that by continuing to read this book, where appropriate and/or necessary, you shall consult a professional (including but not limited to your doctor, attorney, or financial advisor or such other advisor as needed) before using any of the suggested remedies, techniques, or information in this book.

Table of Contents

Introduction

Communications form the core of human relationships. The way you communicate to people in your family, workplace, and society at large goes a long way in determining how they perceive you, and in turn how they relate with you. Each one of us needs to make an effort to master the art of conversation.

Some people have strong social skills, naturally. They have no problem starting a conversation with a stranger, joining a group at a social gathering or even speaking in front of an audience. Others, well, they need a little help. You're here reading this book, so chances are, you're in the category that could do with a little boost.

The good news is that social skills can be developed and nurtured. Here we have gone out of our way to give you information on how you can improve your communication abilities. We start off with the basics of holding a conversation. Have you wanted to walk up to a group of people yet hesitated since you were afraid of not finding anything to say? Here we give you some simple conversation starters that are bound to kick-start a conversation.

It is one thing to have a conversation, and it is quite another to have one that lingers in your mind, and that of others, for years to come. What makes a memorable conversation? We delve into the qualities of such a conversation. We keep them simple enough so you can pick them and practice right away.

Communication is not always fun, sometimes you'll encounter skeptics and individuals that cause you great annoyance. This book prepares you for such situations. You don't have to get overwhelmed and reciprocate the negativity. You can be the bigger person who navigates the situation and ends up unscathed.

Beyond the social setting, the art of conversation is vital in the workplace as well. Working with a team and coordinating them to achieve a common goal is no mean task. Each member of the team has to learn effective listening. Listening seems like such an obvious thing to do, but most of us listen absent-mindedly while also attending to something else. This book teaches you how to listen effectively so that you can grasp the message in its entirety and also leave the speaker feel valued. Several intricacies of communication at work have been explained here. By communicating effectively at all levels, a business enhances its chances of profitability and growth.

Public speaking has not been left out. What makes some people so great in front of an audience while others cringe just at the thought of it? You may be surprised to learn that some of those who seem like 'natural' public speakers have taken years of learning, preparation and practice to get there. And so can you if you take action and find out how to improve your verbal dexterity. One common example everyone knows of it joining a local Toastmasters group. Many famous public speakers gained their skills at Toasmasters.

Chapter 1: Mental Attitude

We all share an internal desire to relate to the world around us. Imagine for a moment, if you could no longer communicate and nobody was able to understand anything that you're trying to tell them. Life would be an unending series of frustrations on your part, mostly. Remove this ability and suddenly life becomes a struggle when nobody can understand your needs and vice versa.

Before you can begin successfully improving your ability to communicate with the people around you, there's something that you need to do first. Your ability to interact with others is going to stem from the experiences you have had in the past, and since experience can be the most effective teacher or all, the experiences of the past are going to impact your communicative ability moving forward. If you can't understand yourself at the most basic level, you can't expect others around you to understand who you are and what you need either.

Effective communication begins with you, and the first place to start is through developing a level of self-awareness about yourself. The ability to reflect on your internal experiences and make sense out of it allows you to accurately process your emotions. This will enable you to determine just how much far your thoughts and emotions are influencing your communication process and the way they affect your nonverbal cues. If you were trying to have a professional conversation but you were in a bad mood over something that happened earlier, having those feelings still coursing through your system is going to negatively impact the conversation you're now trying to have. Your tone might sound harsher than you think, or the annoyance and stress you're feeling might be reflected on in the slight frown between your brows or the downward curve of your mouth. Little signals will be picked up on by the receiving party. Understanding yourself better with the right level of self-awareness might have made you realize that perhaps you were not in the right frame of mind for an effective conversation, and you could have then made the necessary arrangements to postpone it to a better time, or you could have given yourself time to prepare beforehand.

For an effective conversation to take place, emotions must be regulated, and you cannot regulate your emotions without self-awareness. Why is it so important for emotions to be regulated during the communication process? Because our emotions influence our speech and thought process. When you're feeling particularly angry, those emotions might make you perceive the message you're receiving in a different way. What was meant as an innocent remark suddenly gets taken out of context and an argument ensues? A situation that could have easily been avoided if you understood yourself to know that perhaps you were letting your emotions cloud your judgment. An awareness that could have led you to react very differently and produced an entirely different outcome.

To a certain extent, being able to communicate effectively involves emotional intelligence. The five core skills that make up emotional intelligence - **empathy, social skills, self-awareness, self-regulation, and motivation -** are also the core skills that make you a whiz at conversing with just about anyone. Self-awareness and self-regulation give you the skills you need to be able to assess your own emotions, capabilities and then regulate the appropriate action to achieve the most desirable outcome. Empathy and social skills help you connect beyond more than just the surface with the person you're talking to. To be able to put yourself in their shoes, see what they see, feel what they feel, that gives you the valuable insight you need to tailor your messages accordingly. Last but not least, motivation gives you the determination and the drive that you need to stay focused on the bigger picture, to stay focused on why you're having this conversation and what message it is you're trying to deliver.

Without emotional intelligence, making the necessary connection you need with your audience in order to be able to engage them effectively becomes increasingly more difficult. Self-awareness is such a vital part of the communication process and here's an example of why. There will be some people who, despite your best efforts, will prove to be almost impossible to communicate effectively with. You might have family members with whom you can't see eye-to-eye with, no matter how hard you try. You may have colleagues at work with whom you're constantly butting heads with, even though you're trying to best communicate with them to the best of your abilities. As challenging as these people might be, you still **have** to interact with them, it's unavoidable. Self-awareness can be a big help in this instance.

When you know what your strengths are, you can use them to your advantage in the moments when you need to communicate with these challenging individuals. Knowing your own strengths and weaknesses is crucial because once you know the warning signs within yourself, you can then mitigate the potential for arguments to ensue.

The Self-Communication Principle (Intrapersonal Communication)

Before you begin any kind of important speech, you need to be confident about the content you're going to deliver. This process is called **intrapersonal communication, and** it involves having a conversation with yourself. Most people don't realize it, but we already have internal dialogues with ourselves **all the time.** Whether you're doing it consciously or not, the scenarios you play in your mind, the conversations you imagine yourself having, that's all part of the intrapersonal communication that's going on.

The internal monologues we run in our minds are just as important as the external conversations that take place. Communicating with ourselves is an important tool that helps build both our self-perception and self-esteem. The self-talk you have with yourself affects your emotional and mental wellbeing more than you realize. The next time an internal dialogue is happening, tune in and pay close attention to what you are telling yourself. Is the self-communication that's taking place positive? Or does it slant more towards the negative? The latter, of course, is going to drain you of your motivation and your energy levels, robbing you of your self-esteem and confidence in the process if you're constantly focused on your flaws and all the things you can't do. Positive self-talk, on the other hand, can have the complete opposite effect, empowering you and boosting your confidence and self-esteem levels, making you feel like you can conquer any obstacle that comes your way.

Visualization is a strong part of the self-communication principle. Athletes, motivational speakers, and successful individuals rely on visualization to mentally prepare themselves for the performance ahead. Athletes visualize themselves giving their best performance before they head into the game. Motivational speakers imagine themselves in front of a crowd, inspiring the crowd to live their best lives. Successful people visualize themselves achieving their goals. You are now going to apply this same visualization technique by picturing in your mind the way you want a conversation to go **before** you have it.

Chapter 2: What Are Communication Skills?

Communication skills could be described as a set of those vocabulary and non-vocabulary activities that help you relay your intention and emotions to a person. It is an accumulation of all those skills that help you with sending across what you want to do. Your wishes, wants, desires and needs are all carried over to others by usage of communication skills.

Communication signifies an exchange of information from one place to another through a medium. The means could be either natural or artificial. For communication to happen there need be four essentials fulfilled. There has to be at least a sender, a receiver, a medium and a message.

A sender is someone who starts a communication. He is the one in possession of the message initially. He chooses the medium of the transaction and dispatches the message through it. He is the inception of the process called communication. A medium is any means that the sender uses to transmit his message. It could be vocal or in the form of a letter. The medium is that realm wherein the message exists after being sent by the sender.

Message is the core of communication. It is the reason why communication was started in the first place. It is the only thing that shifts place in the whole deal. It travels from the sender to the receiver through the medium. It contains the talked about information and is supposed to reach the receiver. A receiver is the person to whom the message is supposed to reach. He either ends the communication or continues it further by sending a reply to the received message. Usually, receiver is where the communication ends.

Communication skills are varied and ever changing. You may possess a good vocabulary, a baritone to impress the ladies, a talking style that floors the onlookers, an accent to die for, but if you are not a master of communication skills, you are missing out on a really valuable trait.

Communication skills help you not just speak your mind but also know others' as well. It is a constant flow of thoughts and actions that help you channel your emotions and intentions in the best way possible. It enhances your perceptions and improves your responses. When people say 'communication gap', they mean lack of communication skills in the interested parties. It implies that either or both parties had no or negligible amount of communication skills.

Communication skills is a set of mostly verbal traits that help you establish an understanding mental relation with the person you are talking to. It connects you to the other person in better ways than most. Your communication skills also reflect well on your personality.

It takes a lot of practice and patience to master communication skills. Let me warn you here. It is not a child's play to attain the required devotion to master it. Being able to communicate with someone is a desirable trait. When you enhance it to extreme levels, it becomes a valuable asset.

If you are a good communicator, you are being a good people person. Having the right set of communication skills is equivalent to possessing life skills. There must have come many situations in your life that would have required the application of a healthy communication. These situations are so tight that only a trained tongue would be able to bail you out.

When you communicate, you let the other person know that you understand them. You automatically relate to them and no longer make them feel alien. They are comfortable talking to you and won't hesitate to share their dark secrets with you. Communication requires some mastering and mastering takes its own sweet time. The next chapter will deal with the importance of learning communication skills.

Chapter 3: The Importance of Communication Skills

Communication skills do not refer to simply the art of speaking. It signifies something beyond that. Anyone can speak. There are people who are well versed in multiple languages, but not everyone has good communication skills. Being a good communicator requires not just the quality of talking well, but also various incidental traits that supplement it. Being able to listen, make appropriate hand gestures, the right body posture, the right mental wave sending; everything is covered by communication skills.

From a cat to a caterpillar, every creature has its own form of communication skills. You may not have noticed it but animals too have their own structure of communication. Never heard a dog snarl? Or a cat purr? If you learn the right interpretation, they can be broken down to convey numerous animal emotions.

Have you ever found yourself bouncing and idea around and being unable to express it properly? A sudden thought that crossed your mind and you didn't find the right words to give it a name for? Discovered yourself grappling at thoughts that seem to escape your mind as soon as they arrive, only because you couldn't say it properly? Do you have to think a lot before speaking your mind? The reason for this is lack of communication skills.

Communication skills help you express yourself. Everyone has their own ideas, views and suggestions to put forward on the table. But not everyone has the means to express themselves properly. A few words here and there and the entire idea is misconstrued. By the time you form a definite and effective form of the idea that's in your mind, the time for it is long gone.

It helps you establish a mental link with the opposite party. A set of healthy communication skills binds you to the listener. It is vital for communication that the sender and the receiver must be on the same page. If you are talking about the solar system and the receiver is imagining Antarctica, the communication could be at least said to be poor. The link so established between the receiver and the sender has to be strong enough for the message to flow without any special efforts being put in.

Communication skills ease the flow of messages. When you are a good communicator, the efforts you put into communicating are lesser than when you are not. A good communicator always uses the shortest of sentences and the briefest of descriptions. It is a good sign in terms of communication skills that a person is using the minimum possible words. When you are versed with the right skills to communicate, you automatically know what words to choose.

A person with good communication skills naturally improves their own personality. People adore those who are experts in conveying emotions without much effort. Your personality improves tenfold when you are able to talk not just with fluency but also with a rapt audience. An audience decides how good a communicator you are. If you are able to hold your audience, you are one. If you can see people talking among themselves, yawning or picking their noses, there is still some room left for improvement.

The possession of communication skills makes people open doors of possibilities. When you do not communicate well, your options are really limited and short-lived. However, when you are blessed with a good grasp of communication, you know how things work and the right way to put a thing is always right in front of you. You know the pros and cons of saying the wrong words. You are versed with the possible consequences of the wrong coming out of words. You are confident about your business and do not fear any verbal mishap.

It won't be a stretch to claim a person with good communication skills naturally attains the power to influence. The same thing said by person A would sound different coming from person B. The difference lies in the tone, manner and style of conveying the message. Ingredients like politeness of tone, gentlemanliness of speaking and other qualities like the ones mentioned come only from a person qualified in communication. Influencing people is a powerful trait. When you modulate your words to fit the right frequency that exists between you and the targeted person, you are set to influence them to your whims.

It shapes you as a person and differentiates you from others in the community. Communication skills have the power to entirely change the light people see you in.High performance achievers have high communication skills, and you more than likely a "people person" if you are a good communicator.

Chapter 4: Common Obstacles

It is one thing to talk, and quite another to be heard and understood. In most cases, we miss out on the message being communicated simply because we're not listening. We're so accustomed to multi-tasking that we hardly ever attend to just one activity at a time. Listening is no exception. We often lack attention, interest, are distracted or consider the information irrelevant. This forms the first barrier to communication. Somebody is talking, but the listener is not absorbing the information. Other barriers include:

1. Information overload

This happens where there is so much information, and the brain cannot process it all. Think of the many hours you spend online every day. What exactly are you reading or watching? Can you summarize the information you've come across after an hour online? You were clicking one website after the other, watching videos, checking out your friends' profiles on social media and so on. No sooner have you started paying attention to one thing, than you spot a link for something that looks more interesting. You have so much information competing for your attention; you end up absorbing none of it. What a waste of time!

You can prevent this by deciding exactly what it is you need to do online. If you're going to research for a project, stick to that and give yourself a timeline. If you're constantly getting distracted by social media sites such as Facebook and Instagram, you can block them temporarily. If you don't know how to go about blocking them, you're even luckier. Have someone block them for you. You don't know how to unblock them either; right? Good! Now you'll have to do without them. Concentrate on the important matters - actually productive information.

2. Language barriers

You may have encountered this at an international conference. While you may have interpreters for the formal part of the event, informal interactions can get tricky. You find yourself at your lunch table with people from other organizations that you can actually learn something from, yet you can hardly exchange a sentence. Even when some effort has been made to learn the language, accents may still come in the way. You also encounter language barriers when you're an international student, or when visiting another country or continent. If the engagement is only short-term, you can somehow survive. If it's long-term, then learn the language. There are plenty of translation apps, but they mostly work for written content. You may come across a few dealing with the spoken word. You can use them for some time as you hone your new language.

3. Slang and Other Jargon

The use of slang is common in some neighborhoods. Slang is an informal language that is coined randomly, and grow to become accepted language. For instance, missing a class or meeting may be referred to as 'skiving.' The TV is known as 'telly.' 'Cuppa' is used to refer to a cupful – A 'cuppa' coffee. Some of these are distortions of the real words, while others are just made up. One day someone throws in a catchy phrase into a song, next thing you know people have incorporated it into their language.

You may be aware of some of these slang words. To you, they're as correct as any other. To somebody else, they may be incorrect or even strange. Some people will not entertain slang in official communication. Others do not mind. Get to know whom you're dealing with, so that you can communicate in a manner that is deemed fit.

4. Emotional barriers

We often make assumptions about who will listen to us and who will not. Someone going through a rough time fails to communicate believing nobody will care. This must be the reason we have so many people with dark issues which they've bottled inside for years. This may be cases of abuse, rejection, assault, violence, and so on. Communication is hindered by fear of victimization.

Should you happen to be in this category, you do not have to suffer in silence. Keeping things inside will only aggravate the harm. You can talk to someone around you, to your family, friend or colleague. You may be surprised that other people have gone through similar circumstances. If you'd rather talk to a stranger for privacy purposes, there are certified counselors available. Their code of ethics provides for non-disclosure. They say a problem shared is half solved. Just by speaking out, you have made the first step towards healing.

5. Perception differences

One person may perceive an issue different from the other. This is common between men and women. For instance, what may seem like love to a man may not be so with the woman. Sex represents love to a woman, not so to a man. The woman might even assume they're in a relationship and get deeply attached, even making their future plans in her mind. To the man, well, they're just having a good time.

In the workplace, when the boss sends you a memo for the late submission of reports, what does that mean? The boss does not like me? That you'll receive a poor valuation? That you're about to be fired? It could be just what it is; a warning so you can submit on time if the future. The rest could be just your perceptions.

Instead of assuming, you can just speak it out. Ask for clarification. You might act on assumptions only to find out that you were all wrong.

6. Hearing impairments

Every once in a while, you will encounter somebody who is partially and totally deaf. Do you know any sign language? It does not hurt to know the basics. People with disabilities need to be accommodated too. Should you have some in the workplace, the entire team should make an effort to communicate with them. They want to be productive just like anyone else.

Your parents could have partial deafness as they age. You find that you have to shout for them to hear. You can try hearing aid; they're simple external devices that work for most people. Be patient with those with hearing disabilities, remember that in a twist of fate, that could be you.

Successful communication involves talking, hearing and understanding. If any of these steps are compromised, then significant communication has not taken place. In addition to working towards improving conversational skills, we should also eliminate the barriers along the way.

Chapter 5: Difficult People

Difficult people thrive in defying logic; or do they have a different kind of logic? It's hard to tell. While some of them are oblivious to the negative impact of their attitude, others are fully aware of the distress they cause, and it does not bother them much.

Whenever you encounter an unreasonable person, the first instinct tells you to reciprocate the exact same attitude. And why not? They started it anyway, right? This is common in a business where disgruntled customers want to give everyone a piece of their mind. Sometimes they have a legitimate concern. Sometimes not. In fact, they could be in the wrong. Perhaps you should show them that you can yell too, right?

This sounds like an easy approach. However, if you're here reading this book on communication skills, you must be interested in improving your conversation intelligence. You're keen on developing your social skills, improving empathy, learning the art of persuasion and achieving successful relationships all around. Therefore, when you encounter difficult people, you must choose to be the bigger person and deal with the situation rationally.

1.   What's the need?

What is the interlocutor asking for? Listen. Separate the person from the issue. Behind the altercation, there is a real need to be addressed. If a customer is being difficult, perhaps he's been offered poor service or maybe poor quality items. What can you offer? Perhaps you can replace the particular items? Or offer a better service. Perhaps you can even throw in a free item as an apology. On the other hand, you will find that the customer is in the wrong. Maybe he/she is demanding a warranty when the set period has already lapsed.

2. Don't make demands

Once a person begins being unruly, it is tempting to also shout him into submission by ordering him to keep quiet, sit down, calm down, leave and so on. But remember you're dealing with a person who is already agitated. Additional orders will only make matters worse.

3. Involve others

If you're certain that you're in the right, involve other people. If you're at work, call your coworkers. If not, you can involve your family, friends, and even strangers. Maybe somebody else will bring a different approach and the person will listen. If there are more people on your side, even if the person does not agree with you, he's likely to back down.

4. No laughing/smiling

This is not one of those situations where a smile or laughter makes things better. Difficult people do not exactly function like the rest of us do. Trying to appear pleasant will only agitate them further. Maintain a calm and composed face that only signifies that you're doing what you can to remedy the situation.

5. Remain calm

This one is definitely easier said than done. When anger is directed to you, it very quickly stirs anger in you. The problem here is not feeling angry, but letting the anger control your actions. You can control your anger (we have covered that extensively in another topic) and remain calm. Surprise the aggressor who expects you to be equally angry. They will realize that he or she is the only angry one. He/she is likely to calm down on their own volition. Remaining calm also gives you the clarity of thought that you need to evaluate the situation.

6. Disengage

If the person totally refuses to listen, you have the right to disengage and walk away from the negativity. Say something like 'I'll talk to you later when you calm down.' If you're on your premises, have security escort him out.

7. Avoid violence

In worst-case scenario, the person might try to hit or push you. Get away before you're provoked to fight back. You might have come across that video of a McDonald's employee who was pushed by an aggressive customer, and she then turned and attacked him viciously. She had to be restrained by her colleagues. Interestingly, the court found the customer guilty of starting the aggression. She only acted in self-defense, albeit very fiercely. This is what a moment of provocation can do to you. This can happen even to the calmest among us. Walk away quickly before your senses lead you to fight back. You can involve the police if the case meets the threshold.

8. Evaluate the situation

After the situation has calmed down, evaluate it rationally as you destress. Is there something that you could have differently? Was the person behaving that way out of habit or was it an isolated case? What can be done to avoid such scenarios in the future? If you determine that that particular person is inherently difficult and constantly refuses to reason, you can cut out any further contact. You're no dumping site for people's negativity. Protect your space at all costs.

For every difficult person that you deal with without losing your calm, give yourself a tremendous congratulations as that is no easy task. As long as you remain grounded, you emerge as the bigger person. Remember the aggressor will also be evaluating the incident later. They'll most likely feel embarrassed that they were causing all the trouble while you managed to keep calm.

Can difficult people change? Yes, they can. Yes, they should. If you're willing to help, try to seek them out when they're in a good mood. Speak to them about their attitude and actions. They might see some sense. Give them time to go and reflect, and hopefully, they will change with time.

Chapter 6: Dealing with a Skeptic

Skeptics always doubt and question the ideas others put across. They constantly question opinions when they've already been accepted by the majority. Skeptics want proof that the idea is going to work, or a product is going to function as anticipated, or the projections are going to be achieved, and so on.

Communicating with a skeptic wears you out. You don't want somebody who is constantly poking holes in all your ideas. This is far from constructive criticism, which involves pointing out the weak areas and suggestions on how to improve them. Skeptics simply refuse to believe, often without giving a tangible reason.

Skepticism is most difficult to work within the workplace. With a skeptic in your team, you'll hardly get anything done. The arguments go back and forth, wasting time, and not achieving much. What can you do about this?

1. Question

Skeptics are vague in expressing their doubts. 'I just don't like it.' 'The concept doesn't feel right.' 'What if it doesn't work?' Put them to the task of explaining exactly what they're uncomfortable with. 'What exactly don't you like about the concept?' Chances are they'll struggle to answer that. In the process, they'll become conscious of their tendency to question just for the sake of it. Ask them for alternative suggestions. That shifts their mind from questioning to critical thinking. This applies to teamwork, where you're in a group trying to develop an idea. If you encounter such questions when trying to make a sale, seek to know exactly what the prospective buyer is uncomfortable with. They still may not purchase the product, but should they have a legitimate concern, you can take it up and do something about it.

2. Constructive criticism

When working in a team, let there be a specific time for productive criticism. Let the participants know that you can't just barge in and discredit other people's ideas. Don't interrupt the speaker. Wait for your turn. Have an order of presenting ideas: you can start with presentations, then questions, then open the floor for productive criticism.

Every member of the team must use respectful language. One of the ways to achieve this is to use 'I' instead of 'you.' For instance, imagine saying, 'how can you expect the management to approve such a high budget?' Sounds like an accusation, right? But you can say, 'I don't think the management will approve such a high budget.' Exact the same meaning, yet the second one sounds rational and productive. Encourage constructive criticism even when dealing with skeptic clients. 'What don't you like about the product? What improvements would you like to see? What feature can we add?' such questions should help you pinpoint the reasons for their discontent, which can then give you actionable ideas.

3. Use data

Numbers don't lie. Back up your ideas with numbers whenever applicable. Organize your numbers in a manner that is easy to understand. If you're talking about sales in relation to the marketing budget, break them down into monthly results. Include visual aids such as graphs and charts. Let's say you're making such a presentation as a proposal to increase the marketing budget. With such precise numbers, dealing with skeptics will be easier. All you have to do is challenge them with the data. Should they have doubts, they should also present data to demonstrate their point.

4. Add details

Explain everything, including the questions they may have. In fact when preparing to make such a presentation, have the first draft, consider all the questions that arise from that, then include that information in the second draft.

It is not enough to say to a skeptic that 'these pills will help you lose weight.' You have to add more. Come up with something like 'these pills will help you lose 5 pounds within the first month and up to 7 pounds every month after that without dieting. The pills have no side effects.' You can't afford to be sketchy. Cover all the details that you can think of.

5. Call them aside

Have a separate conversation with these skeptics in your team. There are those who are not even conscious of their attitude. They simply think it's their way of contributing to the team. Others are fully aware of their skeptic selves, and get a kick out of antagonizing others. There are also those who are lazy and don't come up with ideas and want to invalidate the ideas of those who make an effort. Point it out to them away from the meeting.

Let them recognize and evaluate their attitudes. Where is the negativity stemming from? Are they dissatisfied with their job? Or the team they work with? Or are they just as a skeptic in other areas of their lives? Point out the harm done by their attitude to the rest of the team. Encourage them to use constructive criticism instead.

6. Nurture positivity in the organization

Set an optimistic standard in the company. This means that the minds of your workers will be focused on the positive in every situation. Instead of pointing out what won't work, they'll point out what will. Instead of doubting ideas, they'll try to build on them and offer solutions. Let them learn diplomatic dialogue, so that they can learn to express their reservations without affecting the cohesion of the team.

7. In social circles

Cynical people are not just in work circles. You will also encounter them among your friends, family, and community. Unlike the workplace where you have to come to a common agreement so that you can execute, out there you don't always have to agree. Imagine telling your peers about a project that you have in mind, and they're skeptical about it. You're not even telling them to get involved. You're just speaking your idea out loud. Here you can simply agree to disagree. You say it can work. They say it can't work. Your views are different from theirs, and that's fine. You can live and let live.

8. Skeptic crowd

It is possible for a crowd to be cynical due to various reasons. This is an audience that assumes it already knows what you want to say, and already doubts it. This is common in politics. Some candidates are dismissed even before they state their case, mostly if they're from minority groups. If you find yourself in such a situation, acknowledge the skepticism and address it. Say something like, 'you may be wondering what an immigrant could possibly offer this county as a governor..' By stating what is on their minds, you capture their attention and they look up to hear your reply.

There will always be skeptics and pessimists in our midst, whether at the workplace, in business, school or even in our families. It's important to note in dealing with such people, one person's definition of success differs from ours and that's fine. The best we can do is to be an inspiration, and really understand that we cannot please everybody.

Don't write off the skeptical people that you come across. You will definitely need to put in some work before they believe in you, but with the above tips, you increase chances. Once they cross that line, you can be assured of their unwavering loyalty.

What if you're the skeptic one? Do you find yourself always second-guessing things that others have already agreed with? Well, you could be a victim. You should be alarmed your conversations always turn to arguments about the merits and demerits of the idea. You should also be alarmed if no one wants to have you in their team. Evaluate the source of your skepticism. Do you have valid reservations, or do you just argue for the sake of it? Imagine how that would feel if you were on the receiving end. You wouldn't like it, right? Make a point of changing your perspective so that you can improve your conversation skills and strengthen your relationships.

Chapter 7: Your Verbal Dexterity

If you Google the most famous speeches in history, you will come across the likes of Martin Luther King, Barrack Obama, Nelson Mandela, Malcolm X, among others. One term can be used to describe the speaking prowess of these world leaders - verbal dexterity. They have mastered the art of delivering speeches. Thousands gather to hear them speak. Their speeches have received millions of views on YouTube, and the numbers continue to grow. You can tell some repeat viewers. They keep watching and listening to them over and over again, stoked by their confidence and eloquence.

Are these speakers different from the rest of us? Were they born pros or did they hone their skills along the way? Well, most of it comes from learning and practice. Some even have teams that help them prepare for weeks or even months before delivering the speech. That's consoling. If they can sharpen their listening skills, so can you. You may not rise to the world stage like they did (and then again, you just might), but you can also speak with conviction in your circle of influence.

Content

The content of these speeches was informed by the activities that these leaders had been involved in for years. Martin Luther King spoke passionately about the civil rights movements and the oppression of the black. These were matters that he has been involved in for years. He knew them by heart. He simply spoke his heart out.

If you aspire to speak as they did, stick to the content that is in your line of work. If you're a teacher, for instance, you'll be better placed to speak about the reforms required in the education center. If you're a nurse, you can draw the attention of the people towards the challenges faced by the health practitioners and patients in the face of unstable health insurance. Go on, find your niche. Mastering that content is a first step in enhancing your verbal dexterity.

Passion

It is one thing to know what is happening in your country or community, and it is quite another to care. Do you have something that you're passionate about? Do you feel the need to stand up for it? Can you do so consistently? It does not have to be confrontational. It just has to be close to your heart. Passion also leads you to get more information. If you're passionate about the need to rid the world of plastic pollution, for instance, you will read through any relevant information. You will be aware of the highest polluting companies, the measures the government is putting in place, any relevant bills, organizations working towards tackling the problem and so on. When you speak on the topic, your speech will be heartfelt, passionate and enlightening.

Once you have these two, the rest is presentation skills that you can learn. Public speaking skills such as stage presence, tonal variation, body language, and technology have been covered in a different chapter in detail. The bottom line is to have the basics in place, then learn and practice the rest.

As exemplified by these leaders, verbal dexterity can change the world. Speaking with passion and conviction gets people to listen to you and heed to your call. Sharpen your verbal dexterity today; the world is waiting to hear your voice.

Chapter 8: Effective Networking

This chapter is for those who spend time in offices or other working environments where the need or opportunities to interact with other people present themselves frequently. We would be discussing briefly about whether you should socialize with your coworkers, and if you should, then how much of it is necessary.

Socializing at the workplace can be important. The reason is that if you belong to the regular working class, then you're spending majority of your awake-time in the office.

You spend 8 hours a day, 40 hours a week, and 2000 hours every year in the office. It is inevitable that you will have to socialize and establish relationships with people at your workplace.

"Socializing with your coworkers is essential for your career," says Alexander Kjerulf. Some reasons why you should consider this advice are:

- Alleviates boredom:

You need other people around you so you can talk to them and alleviate the stress, tiredness or anxiety from within yourself. If you're always glued to your desk, it will not only get you bored, but you'll also end up becoming grumpy and establishing yourself as the "weird guy who never talks to others at the office."

- Increased productivity:

Socializing at the workplace helps create a harmonic environment that ends all kinds of envy and negative competitiveness. This allows everyone at the office to become a unit and a team working for a similar cause. In such an office, employees would still want to be the best or become highlighted, as is evident from human nature, but not at the expense of other co-workers.

Similarly, as an individual, an increased productivity for the group means an increased productivity for you. Knowing that you're not in a hostile environment will help you work better and give the best output that you can.

- It highlights your presence:

Being social in the workplace makes people and hence your higher-ups realize your presence. They see you more often and hence remember you among the many other employees that work for them. This can help you not only get into the good books of your fellow employees, but also of your employers.

In the long-run, this might make the difference between you getting a promotion or being denied that right despite working quite hard at your job.

"So, how much should I socialize at work?"

Now this is a really important question. Always remember that the people at your workplace aren't your real-life friends. They might act like it, but in fact they are just fellow employees who want someone to talk to so that they don't go crazy, just like you do. It's not that they aren't nice people, but whenever jobs and money come into play, true friendship can be obscure.

If your work buddies talk to you at the office quite openly, chances are that they won't after hours. You do not need to have emotional attachments with your fellow co-workers. Now, you might have some great friends at work too with whom you're always hanging out, but exceptions are always there.

<u>Here are a few points that you should always keep in mind while socializing at your work place.</u>

- Know the boundaries:

Knowing the line and making it obvious for everyone is important. You do not wish to do or say something that would make you the talk around office. Establish your boundaries yourself and do not let others or yourself go beyond them.

Again, understand the difference between a friend outside the office and inside. Often, you can crack certain jokes with your outside friends, but office friends might find those jokes highly displeasing.

- Romance and humor:

Romance or inappropriate/controversial humor at the workplace is a big no for anyone who wishes to stick long at their job. If you wish to tell a very cheeky or racist joke, then your office is not the place to do so. You do not want people to think of you as a pervert so acting like one is not a smart choice to make.

Gossip travels real fast, so even if you do manage to hide your office love story for long, it is only a matter of time before everyone at the office would know. And that would make for one awkward tenure at the office for the both of you even if you break up.

- Keep your privacy intact:

Do not indulge into all the private matters of your life with your co-workers. If they ask you about private topics, just steer the conversation away. Your life outside the office and inside it should never mix together.

You need to have a certain amount of trust in your co-workers before indulging into topics about your family, romanticism, religion, views or sex-life. One day, you might be feeling really comfortable talking to a closed-group of people, and the next day everyone knows everything, only with its intensity increased manifold.

- Socialize at your best behavior:

Always socialize with people from the work place when you know you're at your best behavior. We all know what makes us crazy and should avoid interacting with people at such a time.

A good example of this could be of someone who knows that as soon as they have a few drinks, they go wild and end up doing embarrassing stuff. If you are that kind of a person, then ditching the night out for some drinks with the staff might be a reasonable thing to do.

Other people might really be emotional and expressive about a sport. Going with your co-workers to watch a sport for which you have an emotional attachment might make you say something awkward in the heat of the moment. The problem is that your company may not understand your emotional attachment to the game may view you as unstable mentally.

"How to socialize with co-workers?"

Now, here are a few regular opportunities that most of us get at the work place to socialize. You can use these opportunities to gain exposure in the office which would help you create healthy relationships in your workplace.

- **Office hangouts:** we all know about these, and honestly, as boring as they might seem to you, they are actually quite important for your visibility in the office. You do not want to be that guy that's just staring at everyone while they discuss stories from last night's party because you weren't even present there.

- **Happy hours:** some offices organize happy hours for their employees to have an hour or so of relaxation. This is a golden opportunity for office socialization and should be exploited to the maximum.
- **Coffee breaks:** But this is out-ruled for coffee breaks. Learn how to make small talk during this period. Discussing how the work is seemingly endless is an office favorite at most places.
- **Birthday parties:** some offices celebrate birthday parties for employees or company executives as well as company anniversaries. Try playing major roles in these functions. If you're a person who enjoys planning events or is good at it, this is your chance to become an employee with maximum visibility.

Using all the above tips can really turn your work-environment life around for you in the best manner possible. Also remember to target your socialization at important people in the office as this would yield far better results for you in terms of your career. So, try implementing these tips in your life to see some positive results. Who knows, this might just get you a promotion.

Chapter 9: The Importance of Smiling and Appearance

Your appearance is the most important social skill when you are making first impressions.

While it is sad that people can be very superficial, your outward appearance is the first and only thing people see. They have to draw inferences about you right away in order to decide how to proceed with you, so they will make a snap judgement based on how you look.

Therefore, a key social skill involves looking like the kind of person that other people would want to talk to. This does not mean you have to look like a model. On the contrary, you will find that being considered too attractive is intimidating to most people. In reality, you simply want to look clean and approachable. Good hygiene and clean, neat clothes are essential. Keep your hair and/or facial hair groomed and presentable. You can have your own style, but realize that your style communicates a lot about who you are. Wearing loud, flashy colors can make others think you want attention and cannot be taken seriously, while all black can make you appear aloof and too serious.

The color red has actually been shown to make you more attractive to others. While this is not really a social skill, it can play a role in making friends or getting dates. It can also help you land a job if you wear some red to the interview. Try a red dress or shirt or a red accent like a hat or tie. Additionally, red lipstick is always a classy and attractive touch.

Another huge part of your appearance is the expression you wear on your face. Consider the people you see on the commute home from work. The grumpy faces that most people wear do not inspire you to make conversation, right? At the bar, the man who sits in the corner glaring at everyone seems creepy and possibly disturbed, as if he's looking for a fight. The woman who looks like she's on the verge of tears spells drama. The child who smiles at you just makes you want to smile back and say something sweet. You make these inferences about people based on how they look at you, and people make these same inferences about you, and their inferences affect their subsequent interactions with you.

The most open and inviting expression is a smile. A smile accomplishes two things. The first is that it ensures you make eye contact, and the other is that it makes people think you are a warm and friendly person who gives out lots of positivity. This makes people want to talk to you more.

Work on smiling at people as you practice eye contact. It also helps to smile during conversations. The more you smile, the more positive your social interactions should be… it can even make someone else's day. You will notice that you attract more people to you as you smile at them.

It is common to smile at someone and not get a smile in return. Don't take this personally. Just keep smiling. Most people don't smile back because their minds are elsewhere and they do not realize you are smiling at them until it is too late. Others, however, are simply unfriendly. Either way, it is not a reflection of you as a person, so don't let it discourage you from smiling at everyone.

"Resting bitch face" is a joke popularized on social media about women who look "unfriendly" when they are actually perfectly nice and kind people. You may laugh about this "syndrome" unless you are a victim of it yourself. The real reason people have this "syndrome" is that they are not present during social situations and are letting their minds wander instead. The result is a serious, almost mean expression on their face. You can try to focus more in social settings in order to control your facial expressions more closely. Keeping a smile on your face at all times requires a lot of concentration and may not be feasible for everyone, so try doing it when it matters like when you are attending a networking event or are meeting new people at a party.

As you walk around and go through your day, you may find that your real mood manifests on your face. So, if you look angry, irritated, sad, or depressed all of the time, no one will want to talk to you. This is why it's important to force a smile whenever you see someone, regardless of how you feel inside. The very act of smiling has been associated with a release of serotonin, which can enhance your mood.

Smiling is not always a good idea, though. If you are dealing with a situation that requires a large amount of gravity, a smile can show that you are not taking the matter seriously. For example, smiling your way through a funeral or a disciplinary meeting at work can make you look like a jerk.

This is where reading social cues comes into play. People will give you clear cues about what they expect of you and how you should act. You just have to learn how to read these cues. A good basis to start is by reading how other people look. If everyone else is wearing a serious expression and the subject matter is serious, you should opt for a serious expression yourself. If a person starts to talk about a sad or upsetting subject, switch to a facial expression that matches the mood of the conversation. If you notice that other people are glaring at you, consider that you are behaving inappropriately and adjust your facial expression accordingly.

Chapter 10: How to Create Beneficial Conversation

Good social skills hinge on being able to relate and talk to others in a normal fashion. They can also mean the difference between superfluous small talk and warm, meaningful connections. If you want more people to like you, you must learn how to talk to people in a likable way.

The main component to great conversation is empathetic listening. You may be a great listener, but how do you show it? The answer is simply that by being obvious about your empathetic listening, you will excite the other person, proving that you care about what he or she has to say. However, to be an empathetic listener, you must prove that you are listening.

While someone talks, look directly at the person and/or nod and interject with the occasional affirmative motion. When the person pauses, you may mention something directly related to what he or she is saying. Conversely, changing the subject, interrupting, staring into space, and appearing impatient for your turn to talk are all good ways to alienate the talker and ruin the conversation. You want to appear interested by making eye contact and by practicing reflective listening.

Reflective listening refers to the method of repeating back what someone says, showing them that you really did hear what they just said. You may repeat things back verbatim, or, you may rephrase them. Similarly, you may also come back with a reply that proves you were paying attention and are absorbing what the person is saying.

There are different kinds of conversationalists. For example, some just talk forever, never paying attention to social cues causing them to bore and drive other people away. Then, there are wallflowers who don't talk to anyone as they carefully observe their surroundings. Finally, there are confident interactors who enjoy talking to others and listening to their stories with genuine interest. You can see which of the three is the most likable. You want to aim for confident interaction at all times when relating to others.

If you are a shy person, injecting yourself into a conversation can pose a challenge. You may feel inclined to just sit back and listen. While this is great (because listening is the most important foundation of good conversation), you are lacking the other component…talking about yourself. You must be willing to talk as well as listen if you want your conversations to go anywhere. Otherwise, you will bore people and come across as a silent wallflower with nothing to add to the conversation. If this happens, the only people who will talk to you will be the blowhards who talk incessantly and don't know when to shut up. You can avoid these problems by having confident interactions.

The key here is to actually talk to the person you are conversing with. A conversation goes two ways, and you must do your part to keep it going. On top of listening, you should start speaking. Don't just interrupt by blurting out whatever comes to mind or by attempting to change the subject constantly. It's best to actually find relevant topics to bring up.

A relevant topic may be based on what the other person starts talking about. If you want to give the other person control of the conversation, then you can just go along with what he or she talks about. This is a good way to start practicing conversation with people if you are shy.

However, you can also take charge of conversations and propose your own topics. Wait for the other person to stop talking and then bring up a new topic. Possibly find topics that are somehow related to the original one proposed by the other person so that there is logical flow to the conversation.

Starting a conversation first gives you more control of the interaction and allows you to make a solid impression. You can start talking to someone and find ways to relate. Tip: keep mentioning topics until you find one that takes off.

The most relevant topic is one that can bond you and your conversation partner. Finding topics that actually interest both of you is a good way to pass the time without causing boredom or frustration. You will want to find things that you can relate to your conversation partner on, and the more you find in common, the more you will like each other. Briefly introduce yourself and talk about what you enjoy and see if your conversation partner resonates with anything you say.

Asking questions that lead to a person talking about themselves is another way to start a good conversation. Keep the focus on your conversation partner by asking him/her questions about themselves. Ask what he/she likes and for more details about his/her job. Then, if he/she mentions any topic, you should ask them to expand on it. People love to talk about themselves, so this can really encourage a person to open up and like you.

Similarly, you may inadvertently repel conversation and relationships with negativity. For instance, if someone mentions fly fishing and you say, "I hate fly fishing," you are creating a negative factor which can halt the bonding experience. It is far better to stay positive and say something like, "I have never tried fly fishing" or, "I'm not much of a fishing person, to be honest, but I do love being outdoors." Both examples dangle the possibility of still finding something in common in front of your conversation partner, even if you don't enjoy the particular hobby of fly fishing.

It has been found that people who share more and act more intimate or familiar right off the bat tend to make a better impression and make more friends. Therefore, you can actually enjoy more conversational success by acting more familiar with people you have just met. This applies to the warmth factor mentioned earlier. You may feel that this is wrong and that asking personal questions is rude, but people will actually open up to you more if you do.

This idea was proven by an interesting experiment where people were divided into two groups where members were assigned random partners. In one group, the pairs were told to exchange small talk; the other group was told to ask very personal questions from a list. All participants rated how much they liked each other before the experiment and after. The group who exchanged personal questions liked each other the most at the study's end. This is because they were actually able to form a bond and get to know each other.

Naturally, this does not mean that you should ask offensive or upsetting questions, nor will you want to ask someone about his/her religious or political affiliations as this can invite controversy and unpleasantness. Instead, ask personal questions that people might enjoy answering. Your goal is to get someone to divulge information to you so that you can find common ground over which to bond.

You might start conversations with refreshing personal questions that most people don't ask. For example, you might ask someone what he/she would do if they were to find out that they have one day left to live, or what his/her dream job was when he/she was still a kid. You might also consider asking someone about the best book he/she ever read or the most vivid dream he/she ever had. Because questions are not your typical, run of the mill conversation starters, they will intrigue and interest your conversation partner and make for quite dynamic conversation.

Another key to good conversation is to pay careful attention to the ebb and flow of the conversation. If a person starts to withdraw or look bored, don't take it personally. Instead, take it as a sign that you should change the subject. Similarly, if a person starts to get upset, you should definitely change the subject. Consider how to soothe and reassure a person who is not enjoying the topic. Be sure to acknowledge a person's feelings by saying, "I can see this is really important to you" or, "I can see that this upsets you a lot." This kind of emotional recognition makes a person feel validated. Validation is key to being liked.

You are not responsible for how someone feels, but if you want to have good conversation, you should try to keep things pleasant and light. No one really wants to talk about heavy topics, especially if they don't know you well.

Confident interaction involves showing that you are invested and interested. You must listen and you must speak. Maintaining the flow of conversation by going back and forth on relevant topics is the basis of the social skill of good conversation.

Chapter 11: Public Presentation Success

'Is public speaking a natural skill for some and not others?' We constantly ask ourselves every time we watch public figures giving their speeches (or any other presentations) so effortlessly. For most of us, even the mere thought of speaking before an audience is terrifying.

While some are better than others, public speaking can be done by anyone with adequate preparation. Speaking successfully is determined in advance - the preparation stage. It is comforting to know that even those who seem natural at it, like politicians, go through weeks if not months of getting ready.

Here's how a typical preparation stage should look like:

Gather the content: Depending on your audience, come up with the content that best appeals to them. This could be from the library, internet and other forms of archives. Write your speech in the order of introduction, main points than the summary. Writing a speech should not be so casual. Let your personality be felt. If you just put together information from research, there will be nothing unique in that. Anyone can access such information. Add a bit of your personal story regarding your upbringing, education, marriage, career, world views and so on. Blend those experiences into your topics and use them to add depth to your talking points.

Practice: It is one thing to speak in your mind, and quite another to speak aloud. How many times have you prepared your speech, for instance; in a meeting, only to get tongue-tied when your turn to speak arrives? Start by reading the presentation out loud. Eliminate any difficult words that are difficult to pronounce. Start by reading with an even tone, just to internalize the content. Then try reading with the proper tonal variation. Adjust your tone when making strong assertions. Alternate between a hard and a soft voice depending on the content.

Practice in front of an audience of your family and buddies. An imaginary audience denies you the sensation of speaking to people. There are sensations that you go through when people are looking at you with those expectant eyes, waiting to hear what you have to say. That instance can easily leave you in jitters, ruining your opening moment. Speaking to people helps you get ready for the emotions.

What about practicing in front of the mirror? While it is a common option, it is rather distracting. The aim is to see how you appear as you speak, but other things too are likely to catch your attention. Your attention is drawn to how you look, instead of how you speak. The audience is not going to be bothered by those details, so focus on what actually counts.

Get familiar: Getting onto the stage brings a lot of anxiety. Even experienced speakers will tell you that those first few moments after getting on stage are hard. If you can visit the venue beforehand, do so and practice. Pictures and videos will do if you're far away. Study them until the venue feels familiar to you, like a place that you visit often. Have a look at the stage. How big is it? Which side does it face? Which side will you enter from? Will the microphone be fixed or portable? Which form of visual aid will work best? You may have planned a dramatic speech with lots of movement, only to find the microphone is fixed and you have to stand on the lectern the whole time. Acquainting yourself with the stage helps boost your confidence.

Comfortable Attire: Your dress code is what first impressions are all about. If any bit of your attire is uncomfortable, it will distract you from your core mandate of delivering a message. This especially goes for ladies. Is your skirt/dress too short when you sit? Remember you might be sitting at the front facing the audience. You don't want to keep pulling it down. Adjusting your clothes constantly reflects poorly on your confidence. Cover up appropriately in decent formal wear. Nothing too catchy, as the attention of the audience might be distracted. The men will do with a well-fitting suit.

When the day comes, arrive early. All the preparation above can be wasted if you get there late. To begin with, you'll be anxious, and anxiety clouds your thoughts. Arriving late also reflects badly on the audience. Punctuality always makes a good first impression.

1. Catchy opening

You're finally on stage for the long-awaited presentation. How does that feel? Having prepared with the tips above, chances are you're confident and rearing to go. The audience is waiting with bated breath. Your opening statement is like that first bite of a meal, it forms a permanent perception. Start with something personal, or a joke in good taste. In a different chapter where we discussed the use of humor in conversation, we agreed that opinion is divided regarding the use of jokes to start presentations. What is the worst that can happen? The joke can flop, and you'll have started on a low note.

However, you do not have to wait to coin or test the joke there. You can prepare it in advance. That's right; jokes are often prepared in advance, even those made to sound like they've just been composed in the spur of the moment. If you can open with a funny joke, you're off to a good start. A personal story also grabs the attention of the listeners and gives them a personal attachment to you. Set a high momentum right from the start and the audience will be hanging on to your every word.

2. Body language

What you portray with your body is just as important as what you say. Move around the stage as space allows. This shows you're relaxed and confident. Stand with your feet slightly apart. Use appropriate gestures. Make random eye contacts. Not too long though; you don't want to make anyone uncomfortable. Your eyes should be trained right above their heads. When you look at the audience at that angle, it looks like eye contact from down there. Speak slowly. We're referring to the pace here, not the volume. Rushing over your content makes you sound nervous. Project your voice with clarity. Let the volume of the microphone be adjusted if you feel like you have to shout. Vary your tone appropriately throughout the speech. Let your body language be in tandem with your words.

3. Show confidence

It is one thing to be confident, and quite another to show it. Can the listeners tell that you're confident? That will inform their expectations. There are those speakers that make a poor first impression and are dismissed from the start. You can see it in the demeanor of the listeners. They sink back into their chairs and look bored. Such a speaker will have a hard time salvaging the situation.

How people perceive you affect how you behave. If the listeners sit up and look eager when you begin to speak, you'll feel energized to do just that. Once you portray confidence from the onset, you raise the expectation, and that perception bounces right back to you.

Enjoy yourself as well. Be excited about the opportunity to speak and the topic at hand. Speak with enthusiasm. Smile. Once you radiate these traits, the crowd will follow suit to the end. Make sure that you have some actionable points at the end, something the listeners can go try out on their own.

Along with knowing what to do, is also knowing what not to do. One of the most common mistakes speakers make is talking "down" on the audience. Speakers are generally considered to be experts, right? Let's say you're an expert in lifestyle diseases. You want to tell your audience that their lifestyle and diet choices increase their risk of disease. You have to say it reasonably, without criticizing them. Don't say something like, 'when is the last time you had some exercise? You can't expect to live long the way you are now!' To you, it might sound like a motivation to initiate change, but it sounds plain offensive to others.

Avoid too many numbers, which is referred to as data-centric content. Some speakers are of the opinion that numbers equal intelligence. They present statistics after another, each with a larger number than the last. Unfortunately, such a strategy does not work. The listeners will quickly lose interest.

It's your human story that people connect to, not figures. Tell them how your topic affects their lives. Give them snippets of your own life, discuss common human challenges. Suggest solutions that people can work on together. You may point out the negatives, but don't dwell on them. Nobody wants a presentation that sounds like one long rant. Give people hope. That is what the human heart yearns for. Optimism is in short supply around us. Be a generous supplier. Once you set yourself apart as a speaker who leaves people feeling better than he found them, you can be sure they will want to listen to you time and again.

Chapter 12: Build a Good Personality

What do people mean when they say that you have a good personality? Mostly they mean that you're warm, likable, and a pleasure to be around. Personality is basically the thinking and behavior pattern that makes one unique.

Just as we alter or improve our physical appearance to get to a certain standard that we deem attractive, so can we improve our personality. In fact, we should put more emphasis on personality as opposed to physical traits. As far as opportunities are concerned, looks will get you through the door, but it is the personality to keep you there. Research done among fortune 500 CEOs shows that their main consideration when hiring, after the experience, is personality.

Your personality determines your ability to communicate with those around you and eventually form lasting relationships. Here's how you can improve your personality.

1. Better listening

Listening seems like such an obvious activity that we all do even without a second thought. However, most of us are doing it wrong. We only half listen as we attend to other matters or browse on our phones. Effective listening involves paying full attention to the speaker in the present moment. Look up, turn the body towards the speaker. Maintain eye contact. Nod along the way. Restate and ask questions where necessary. It is not enough to be listening; it is just as important for the listener to know that you're listening.

In a world so accustomed to multitasking, you stand out when you listen attentively. People will gravitate towards you since your listening makes them feel valued and appreciated. They will be encouraged to open up, knowing that you're taking in every detail. Such are the conversations that make an impact.

2. Stay informed

It is one thing to have the ability to say something, and it's quite another to have something valuable to say. Maybe the ability to communicate comes easily to you. You're confident enough to speak in various spheres. However, do you have the content to match? People get bored with shallow talk really fast. They will be drawn by your speaking ability but will lose interest as so as they learn that you have nothing meaningful to say.

We're in the age of information, with so much of it at the palm of our hands. Yet even then, you have to make a conscious decision to go for the right information. Instead of spending hours online browsing through the profiles of friends, foes, and celebrities, endeavor to teach yourself something meaningful. Keep abreast of current affairs. Dig out the new trends in your industry. Study what is happening in politics, business, sports, entertainment and any other field of interest.

No matter what direction the conversation takes, you'll have something to say. You'll have an opinion. Your arguments will be informative and intellectually stimulating. People will listen to you and learn something new.

3. Positive attitude

Nobody wants to listen to a whiner. Even if things are actually bad, we don't want to keep being reminded. If you're not happy with the boss, or your mother-in-law, or the traffic, or the status of your bank account, you don't have to moan about them all day long. Most people will utilize the first chance to get away from you, while those who will stay and listen will not help you at all. If you actually have grievances like we all do, direct them to the relevant entities who can do something about them.

Look for something positive to say in conversation; such as, Compliments, appreciation, enncouragment, giving hope. **Do** Point out the positives even in a difficult situation. With so much negativity around us, your positive attitude will be a welcome break, and everybody who meets you will be glad they did.

4. Grooming

Your dressing and body physique makes a first impression. People will have an opinion of you even before you get a word out of your mouth. Grooming comes easy for some. They have an eye for style. They can put together a splendid outfit without much effort. Then we have, well, the rest. They throw on the first thing they find in the morning. Or whatever they haven't worn in a while. Or the only clean clothes they got. These are people who have had the same haircut for years. And don't know the price of a manicure.

Please note that poor grooming does not mean that you're a terrible person. You could be an excellent performer at work, a productive member of society and doting to your family. Those who know you might overlook your grooming, but remember they're only a small group. The rest of us judge the book by the cover.

Declutter your closet and throw out those flabby clothes. Get shopping. If shopping is not your thing, you can enlist the help of a stylist. Stylists can take your measurements and shop even in your absence. Get a new haircut. Perhaps some color in your hair would also look good, too. A manicure and pedicure could come in handy too. Get moving if you're out of shape. Once your first impression speaks highly of you, you attract the right attention that leads to productive conversations.

5. Outgoing

Go out and meet new people. Know their cultures, languages, beliefs, habits, and so on. If you had any prejudices against people of a different background, you may be surprised how misleading they could be.

Meeting and interacting with people of different backgrounds teaches you that we're all just human.

An outgoing personality will make you more empathetic and tolerant. You will then be in a position to converse comfortably with people from diverse backgrounds.

6. Confidence

We saved the best for last. Confidence is a trait that will get you through many doors. A confident person is regarded as competent and skilled. Some people are naturally confident, others not quite. If you fall into the second category, you will be glad to know that confidence can actually be nurtured. Walk with your head high. Shake hands firmly. Project your voice with clarity when you speak. Master your content so you're saying the right thing. Hone your public speaking skills. Confidence attracts people to you, and the conversations you have lead to great relationships.

Chapter 13: The Secrets of Successful People

Every time that we see a movie star on an interview or a successful person on TV, we see that they have what most of us don't, likeability. People love and admire them, and all wish they could be their friends. We want to be like them, but where can we start?

Sadly, there isn't an easy way to be successful. People are loved and liked for different things, and there isn't a catch-all answer that you can apply to every situation. However, there are steps that you can take to be successful and create a better version of yourself.

Being better is a work in progress. You have to understand that practicing every day is what made them the people that we admire today. Whether we are talking about George Clooney or Jeff Bezos, you can bet that they share many habits, and while the details might be different depending on their business, they all follow the same basis.

1-   Always set a goal

What is your goal? What is your passion? What do you love, and why? These questions should be your first step. What do you want to be? Do you want to be an actor? A successful businessman? Or perhaps you want to be a politician so you can fight for the greater good?

Your answers should be yours, write them down. Write down an essay on why you want to be that sort of person, and how are you going to do it. Put them where you can see it every day, like on a board in clear view, for example. Set down your goals and ask yourself how you are going to achieve them. If you want to become a movie star, you will have to start with the basics - acting classes. If you want to be an innovator like Steve Jobs, start by studying and reading everything you can about the subject that you love. Always push yourself a little more, and never settle for mediocrity.

When you take classes on whatever you want to study, don't just leave it at that. If acting is what you want to do, watch videos on YouTube, read books about it, go to castings, get a camera, and record yourself doing a soliloquist. It doesn't matter if it is horrible because you have to understand that your current talent will always be worse than your talent tomorrow. Always strive to be better, and you are under no obligation to be the same person that you were the day before.

2-   Be Proactive

You have your goal set, and you have decided the best way to reach it, so you decide to start tomorrow. However, you wake up that day and leave all your work for the next day. And so on and so forth for an entire month. If you are looking for success to come out of nowhere, the chances of that happening are even smaller than getting hit by an airplane while sharks are raining from the sky. Joking aside, success only comes to people who look for it. It doesn't have to be right away, and it will take time and effort. That's the hard part and the one where most people quit and decide that success isn't for them. You will have to make sacrifices, and you will have to push you and your team (if you have one) to the point of no return.

When you are learning how to do a certain task, don't just stay stuck on one idea. Go out and learn everything you can. Take notes of every book you read and every movie you see. Inspiration will come from places that you cannot see yet.

Remember - successful people improve their lives by making the most of their day and staying focused on a desirable outcome or goal. Unsuccessful people only react to whatever life throws at them. They can't be bothered to understand what they have to do in order to improve themselves. Don't be that kind of person. You can be better. You have to be better. You will be better.

3-   Exercise

Have you noticed that no matter what field they are in, successful people always pay attention to their health and diet? They aren't overweight, they are fit, and they look their best. Whenever we see one of those titans sick or under huge distress, we are surprised. While it is true that up to a certain point, they can control their image and what is published online, they can't control everything, no matter how hard they try.

They pay attention to their diet and spend hundreds of dollars to eat the best food available. Of course, we cannot be expected to do it right as we set our goal to be the best version of ourselves, but we can change our habits. How many times do you eat fast food a week? Can you reduce it? Eating healthy isn't that expensive, no matter what you might be thinking. Before starting to exercise or changing diets, always talk to your doctor, as they will recommend you small steps to do it.

If your doctor allows you to exercise, my personal recommendation is to get a gym membership. But if money is tight, you can go out for a run around the park. Try to do some exercise at home three times a week. Don't leave it for tomorrow. Tomorrow is now, and you have to work out.

Once you have a routine, try to adapt your life to it. If you decide to work out in the morning, wake up earlier to do so, and set your time accordingly. However, no matter how good your routine is, it will fail if you are not consistent. If you set a goal, do it. Don't make excuses or blame others, and practice will make you perfect. It will be hard, but every successful person in the world has invested hundreds of hours creating and shaping their body and soul.

4-   Take responsibility not just for your success but also for your failures

The titans of the industry have one thing in common - they learned from their mistakes. It doesn't matter if someone else was at fault when it comes to a mistake, they had their share of responsibility, and they own it. Learn from your mistakes, because only in mistakes do we see our true self. We cannot strive to greatness and become fantastic people if we always succeed.

Failure puts us against the ropes, and it will do everything in its power to knock us down.

Learn from your mistake, admit that you made it, and people will take you seriously. On the other hand, if you point fingers and blame others, people will think that you are immature. When you see someone that always puts the blame on others, you start to believe that they cannot be trusted because in the future, when something goes wrong, that person may betray you and blame you for all the mistakes. Keep in mind that you are the only person that can be responsible for your own success.

5- Be Punctual

Punctuality is a skill that will greatly improve your life and reputation. Time is the only thing that we cannot gain. Once time is wasted, it cannot be earned, so you must make the most of it.

Be aware that, as precious as time is for you, the same can be said for your friends or business partners. They cherish their time, just like you, so don't leave them waiting for your presence. Always arrive fifteen minutes earlier to any meeting. If they make you wait, listen to their excuses. It is normal not to arrive on time once or twice. However, if your friend always has an excuse, then perhaps the best thing to do is to tell them how much it bothers you. Remember what we talked about earlier? Always express your problems and conflicts, but do so politely. If you do not do this, people will believe that you will wait for them no matter how late they are.

When it comes to your work and business-related deals, always be aware of your deadline. Don't ever leave whatever project you have to do to the last minute. Prepare it with enough time, and divide your tasks in smaller chunks to see if you can tackle them faster. Delegate important tasks to people you trust. Your customer pays for your time, so you don't want to let them down. Of course, sometimes life can get in the way; for example, while I was writing an article, my father got very sick, and I had to delay my delivery to focus on my father. Luckily, the client understood and gave me enough time to do both things. At the end of the day, my father got better, my client was satisfied that I was honest, and all went well.

6- Control your emotions

We mentioned this in another section of the book, but it doesn't hurt to repeat it: You cannot, under any circumstance, allow your emotions to get the best of you. No matter what happens, you have to calm down and keep them under control. Sure, you may feel like shouting, but if you want to be successful and a great leader, your emotions will get in the way.

Most people are controlled by their emotions. They act with their emotions, not with their intentional minds. Don't let your emotions control you. If you have to fire someone, don't do it because you are angry. We always see that in Hollywood movies - the nonsense boss who doesn't get what he wants and fires the first person who enters the room. While I'm sure it is based on a real-life boss, the reality is that no successful person is like that. I can't imagine Jeff Bezos doing it because Amazon shares dropped 1% that year, or Elon Musk after a failure to launch a rocket. One thing to add to all of this is that they respond to shareholders, and their perception of the CEO's ability to deal with his emotions is important for the future of the company.

While in our lives we don't have to deal with shareholders controlling each and every move we make, on the news, we always see people who cannot control their emotions. For example, how many times have you seen an act of road rage that escalated to the point that the police had to get involved? Those people aren't stable and allow their emotions to cloud their judgment. Most of the time, those very same people are the first who say that they regret what they did.

Keep your cool, and your emotions in check.

7-   Prioritize your tasks

You might think that those who accomplish a lot always have a massive task list to get done, but the truth is that they focus on ONE task alone, *and they dedicate enough time to see it through to the end*. When they see that they can delegate a task, they get the best person possible to do it and allow them to tackle the problem. But this doesn't mean that they forget about it. On the contrary, they are back to check their progress in no time.

This is the secret of prioritization of tasks. <u>You deal with one thing at a time, and then go on to the next thing.</u> If you do everything at the same time, you won't finish anything. This applies to all aspects of your life. If you want to learn a new language, don't do it at the same time that you are driving to work. Focus on one task at a time. This doesn't mean that you cannot multitask. But if you try to cook and watch TV at the same time, you won't be able to do any of those to a satisfactory level.

Most of the time, the average person attends their task at the last minute. They leave it because they focus on the most enjoyable task first, and then realize that they don't have enough time to do it, or leave it for the next day, and the tasks keep adding up. After a while, there are so many tasks that they can't do anything, they reach a paralysis stage of inaction.

8-   Focus your mind on improvement

At the end of the year, you will see lists like "The Books that I Loved This Year" (or something along those lines) published everywhere. If you ever take the time to read them, you will see that successful people read almost anything. From sci-fi to historical drama, they read every book that they find interesting.

This is something that always spiked my interest, and after trying it for a while, I realized why they do that, and it is because they want to be better at different things. We talked about how inspiration can come from different places, and that's the truth for them. They see every improvement, no matter how small, as a way to get to their goal. If they exercise (which all of them do), they see that every little bit of progress is far better than doing nothing and complaining.

If you aren't happy with your life and your situation, you can change it. Focus on what you can change, and confront what you can't. Nobody is going to knock on your door and say "here, you ordered success, sign here please". You must go out and face reality. You have it in you to do it.

We tend to believe that successful people all have high IQs (Intelligence Quotient), that destiny, God or the Universe decided that those special people are going to lead the way in several subjects, and break off the mold, or that they will tear down the walls of progress and make their own way.

Well… this is not the truth. Or at least, not the entire truth. According to several studies, there might be an advantage to not being a genius. While a certain level of IQ is obviously beneficial, you don't have to be a super genius like Einstein to achieve success.

When you study chess players, for example, your preconceptions will indicate that the higher the IQ, the better player they are. However, there have been several cases where the younger, inexperienced players (who felt like they didn't have as high an IQ as the more experienced player) always try new things or new plays and work twice as hard to master the basics. However, their rivals, being overconfident, didn't try as hard as they should have. This happens at every level of our lives, from business to sports. There is always the risk of not paying attention to a task, and more experienced people are prone to doing so. If you want to be successful, and become like the titans in business, always tackle problems with your full attention and deal with them with enough responsibility. It doesn't matter if you have done it 20 times in the past six years. Deal with it like it's the first time. Be strong, safe, honest, and direct.

Another factor that makes successful individuals stand out from the rest is their ability to comprehend and understand people and their attitudes. We previously talked about the power of interpersonal skills and how they impact a person's success, and because of this, we can infer that PQ (or 'people intelligence') is more important than IQ, at least when it comes to social skills and dealing with people.

If you ever asked yourself how well you work with others, and you took a long while to answer, then you probably aren't a people person, so you should focus on improving your skills and creating better bonds (which you are already doing if you have reached this point in the book!).

But once you realize that you can improve, and that 'Much to learn you still have' (like Master Yoda would say), the next step should be to become a master with 1o.ooo hours under your belt in any particular subject. Constant practice is the key to success, and if you want to become great, you have to dedicate several hours a week to reach that 10.000 hours mark.

Yes, it sounds like a lot of work, but that's what separates successful people from the rest. They made an effort to get there and become better, even when they were in pain. They have discipline, and they put in the hours that it takes to achieve mastery. They go beyond what is expected of them, so why wouldn't you?

The most successful people in the world embrace failure and use it as a starter point. Why? Because failing means that you can still learn, and learning is the best way to improve. It is in failure that we see our true self, and how we react to it will determine if it is a failure or just a minor setback.

When you fail, you will want to know what you did wrong. Write down your failures and critically evaluate what caused them. Create and brainstorm on ideas to avoid doing it again. Save those ideas, learn from them, and use them to turn your mistakes around. One quick way to do so is to find a mentor.

A close friend can help you see where you failed, make your ideas better, and push you in the right direction. They will hold you accountable, and you can write down a schedule to see the progress on your success, creating a timetable with several steps to push yourself. Adhere to that timetable, and you will see that this is one thing that you will have in common with the best in the industry. For example, Steve Jobs had Steve Wozniak, and they both created Apple together. Also, a mentor will keep you in check and warn you when you are veering outside your own path and will teach you from their experience in similar situations. This is an invaluable tool to become successful. They can be hard on you, but that doesn't matter. What truly matters is that they want success for you.

Body language is another important thing to know because your body will express more things that you can say with words. No matter how much you practice a specific subject, or how much your mentor pushes you, unless you can express and exude confidence with your body, nobody will take you seriously. All winners and losers have different body languages. From the alpha of the pack to the beta, they stand differently, and people thus treat them differently.

The true body language of a winner is to roll your shoulders back, open your chest, plant your feet, and always keep your head up. Look everyone in the eyes, and address them directly, with a safe and secure voice. This is the 'High Body Power' technique, commonly known as the technology that allows you to "take up space around you with your body"

If you master these skills, in time, no one will be able to stop you. All of the above skills have a direct correlation with effective communications.

Ending summary

Being able to communication with others effectively applies to all positive aspects of your life, such as; career, business success, family relations, associates, sales, talking to your kids, writing, copywriting, journaling, blogging, etc.

This ONE skill can have a great impact on your life if you master it and become good at it. Practive makes perfect, start by implementing the positive actions suggested in this book and practicing speaking outloud by yourself or in front of a mirror.

You can also make a YouTube channel and make videos of your speeches, keep the videos private for your review only, or make them public. Focus on something you are passionate about so that your natural charisma will come out.

There are other factors that go into this, body language, facial expressions, word selections, attire, eye contact, etc.

You have already started your first steps in changing your life. I hope this book was able to help you understand why we feel anxiety and stress in social situations. You have also completed these simple lessons that will guide you for a lifetime. These steps will take practice, patience, and an open mind to achieve.

The next step is to change another part of your life that has been hindering your happiness and self-development. For example, it may be to quit smoking in order to better your health.

It might be losing weight and exercising – leading to you running your first marathon. It can be you learning a new language and then moving and living in a new country.

It can be you quitting your job and starting a new career in something you love! You can achieve anything you set your mind to. Life is full of surprises. You never know what one can achieve if one doesn't try.

<u>Helpful Links and Resources</u>

- https://www.thebalancecareers.com/communication-skills-list-2063779

- https://www.skillsyouneed.com/ips/communication-skills.html

- http://www.careerizma.com/skills/communication-skills/

- https://www.britishcouncil.co.ke/programmes/education/business-english/workplace-communication

9 781709 133039